Prudent K9 Training Lifestyle Handbook

Table of Contents

About Me

Hi, I'm Seth.

I first discovered my passion for dog training while working through issues with my Chow/Lab mix, Bear. Later, I honed my skills and tackled new challenges with my German Shepherd, Kilo. However, soon after teaching my own dogs everything I thought they should know I found I was still eager to keep training.

I sought to train dogs with different issues and signed up to foster for a local animal rescue. Fostering provided me with the unique opportunity to grow as a trainer and aid misguided dogs on their paths to their forever homes. They taught me, and continue to teach me, how to best meet their needs using strong leadership, structure, clear expectations and accountability.

When I started, I set out to use pure-positive methods: rewarding good behaviors and ignoring bad behaviors. However, very quickly I found myself following my dog's lead as I waited for my dog to offer me behaviors I wanted or voluntarily stop behaviors I did not want. These methods left me with no control and miserable.

My distress and frustration led me down a path to find what actually worked for me. After countless hours of research, studying and hands-on experience, I adopted a practical approach to dog training. This approach empowered me to lead them in a way they understood, enriched my relationship with them and, overall, made life much more enjoyable for all of us.

The approach was relatively simple. I presented myself to my dogs as a confident leader, someone to respect and follow. I gave them structure for predictability by providing them with food, shelter, and security. I offered clear expectations so they knew which behaviors were permissible and which were unacceptable. Finally, I presented consistent consequences for good and bad behavior by providing the follow-through that made my leadership believable.

The discovery of my passion for dog training further encouraged me to share my knowledge. I wanted everyone to experience the feeling I had when it all clicked for me and I took the reins to redefine my relationship with my dogs. I started Prudent K9 Training with the mission to help as many owners and dogs as I possibly can. I want to rehabilitate and train dogs and empower their owners. I want to impart the knowledge and skills on owners and their dogs to have the best relationships possible.

Introduction

Prudent K9 Training provides immersive lifestyle training for dogs; shifting their perspectives, changing their behaviors, and empowering their relationships with their families. This is the emphasis of my Board and Train program and through this handbook I will share with you the substance behind it that makes it all work.

My goal is to share my philosophy and associated methods with you, so you can incorporate them into your own life for continued success in establishing and maintaining a healthy, well-balanced relationship with your dog.

Philosophy

Lifestyle training for dogs is the concept of teaching dogs the mindset, skills, and behaviors required to maximize their inclusion in our lives. Ultimately, the more we are able to integrate our dogs in our lives, the more fulfilling our relationships with our dogs will be.

Lifestyle training is accomplished by focusing on changing dogs' perspectives and behaviors. Our job is to redefine what dogs view as acceptable and unacceptable based on our determination. After establishing the rules the dogs will live by, we enforce them to change their behaviors.

Lifestyle training results in the empowerment of our relationships with our dogs. The hard work and effort we put into changing our dogs' perspectives and behaviors produces dogs that are well-adjusted and fit seamlessly into our lives. The training allows us to create dogs we envisioned that add significant value and minimal stress to our lives.

Lifestyle training is built on the foundation of leadership, structure, rules, accountability, and consistency. The following sections will expand upon each topic and give you a clearer understanding of what it takes to establish a healthy relationship with your dog.

Leadership

We have leaders that guide us in the right direction in our lives and dogs require the same; arguably more so given that they are dogs in a human world. Our dogs need a leader to teach them and help them navigate through the life we have given them. We have accepted this position by bringing dogs into our homes and we owe it to them to fulfill this need of theirs to the best of our ability. If we do not lead our dogs they will try to navigate our world with their own natural instincts and that will almost certainly guarantee their failure.

The cornerstone of your relationship with your dog is leadership, so naturally, the first task in establishing a healthy relationship with your dog is to become your dog's leader. Becoming your dog's leader begins the moment you decide who you are, what you do, what you want, where you are going, how to get there, what you expect of others, and how to communicate this information clearly and effectively. The confidence that comes from making these decisions serves as the foundation to lead yourself and your dog and enables you to take purposeful action toward your goals.

As your dog's leader you are in control, firm and fair. You make the best decisions for yourself and your dog. You serve as a source of guidance and direction for your dog and your dog will look to you when he or she is unsure. When your dog requires correction, it is your responsibility to provide it consistently without anger. Your leadership is the first step in setting your dog up for success.

Structure

Structure refers to how you design your dog's daily agenda, your daily routine. The goal is to establish a consistent routine that accounts for every moment of your dog's day. There is not a one size fits all routine that all dogs must follow. The ideal routine is one that is personalized to meet the needs of you and your dog.

Before you overwhelm yourself considering how you will fill your days with high energy activities while still holding down a job, please remember that crating your dog and exercising your dog are both activities that will fill your dog's day; one is just a high energy activity and the other is a no energy activity.

When designing your routine, remember that your dog needs to adapt to your lifestyle and not the other way around unless your dog is a puppy, injured, or ill. If letting the dog out at 6 a.m. every morning doesn't work for you because you do not wake up until 7 a.m., then design your routine around that. Dogs are amazingly adaptable and will adopt whatever routine you create and consistently stick to.

Establishing routine is a great way to create predictability in our dogs' lives. Nervousness and uncertainty can come from an unstructured environment where the dog does not know what is coming next and is constantly on edge. A daily structured routine gives them a sense of security because they know what to expect and there is less opportunity for them to panic about unknowns.

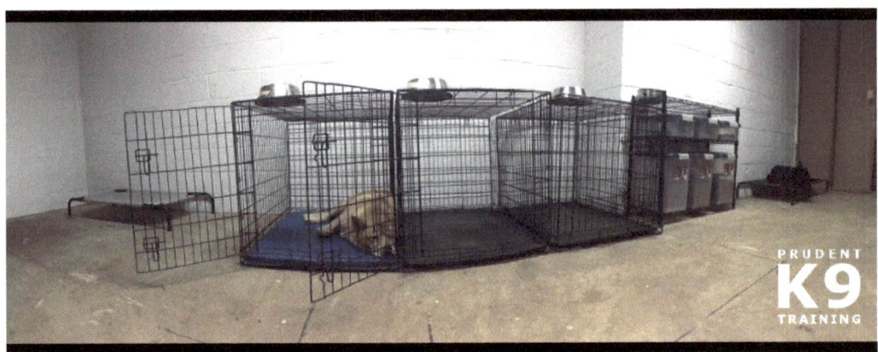

Rules

Dogs require rules to meet our expectations. Dogs will not know which behaviors we allow or disallow until we make it clear to them. They only know what works for them and default to behaviors that fulfill their desires. Many of these instinctual behaviors will not be acceptable to us. Many examples of this come to mind, so let's look at a few:

- Your dog needs to relieve himself and does so on your living room rug.

- Your dog hears a knock on the door and proceeds to address the perceived threat by barking excessively and charging the door.
- Your dog smells something enticing in your trashcan and proceeds to knock it over, spilling garbage across your floor and eating whatever sparked his interest.

As you can see, what a dog naturally wants to do is not always acceptable behavior in our world. It is okay that they do not naturally do what we want because they have no idea what that is until we establish rules that allow them to meet our expectations for their behavior.

It is our responsibility to establish clear expectations of appropriate behavior so our dogs understand what behaviors are expected of them. Teach your dog your rules so they know what you want and don't want. Be consistent to make it as easy as possible for your dog to understand your rules. Don't accidentally confuse them with rules that are enforced inconsistently.

Accountability

Once we establish rules for our dogs' behaviors and our dogs understand what we expect of them, we have to hold them accountable for their actions. We use consequences to create accountability. A consequence can be good or bad. We simply reward desired behaviors and punish unwanted behaviors.

When your dog does something you want, you want to communicate that clearly to the dog. You do this by giving your dog a reward. Your reward can be verbal praise, physical touch, food, a toy, or an activity. It can be one or all of these, whichever is appropriate for the given situation. Clearly communicating to your dog which behavior was right using a reward will increase the likelihood of your dog repeating that behavior.

When your dog does something you don't want, you want to clearly communicate to your dog that the behavior is unwanted. You do this by using punishment. Punishment can be the removal of something they want, such as your attention, presence, or affection, or a desired object such as a toy or food.

Punishment can also be presenting something they don't like as a consequence for the unwanted behavior. Punishments that work this way are audible corrections (e.g., verbal, loud clap, shaking coins in a can), leash pop corrections, eCollar corrections, pet convincer and bonker corrections. Clearly communicating to your dog what was done wrong using a punishment will decrease the likelihood of your dog repeating that behavior.

Being fair and consistent with your rewards and punishments solidifies the rules you have established to regulate your dog's behaviors. It is important to hold your dog accountable for their actions because without accountability your dog will never fully understand your rules and the associated expectations you have for your dog's behavior.

Consistency

The real heavy lift in dog training is being consistent over time. Consistency applies to everything that has been discussed: leadership, structure, rules and accountability. This commitment to be consistent over time is the piece that takes the most work but undoubtedly yields the greatest results.

Drastic changes can occur very fast using the right techniques and tools, but lasting change takes time. If we want our dogs to clearly understand and meet our expectations we have to offer them consistency; consistency in what we ask of them and consistency in the delivery of positive and negative consequences throughout our dogs' lives. Training is not just obedience commands and tricks; it is a lifestyle which encompasses all aspects of the dog's life.

Health

Much of my attention in this handbook is focused on behavior, but I do not want to discount the importance of your dog's health. Your dog's health, including nutrition and exercise, is a critical component to a well-balanced dog.

First, your dog should have a good veterinarian. Find a veterinarian that you have confidence in and are comfortable with talking to about any health issues your dog may experience. A good relationship with your veterinarian enables you to address health issues as soon as they arise for the best possible outcome. Keep regular visits and keep your dog up to date on all shots and vaccinations.

Second, your dog should have a well-balanced diet. Ideally, we would feed our dog the most organic, raw diet available, but that is not practical for everyone. Just feed your dog the best dog food that you are able to provide. Find a good brand of dog food and ensure you provide your dog the appropriate amount for their size and weight. Do not overfeed your dog and do not feed them table scraps!

Third, but most importantly, exercise your dog! Ensure your dog receives the appropriate amount of exercise required to match your dog's energy level. All dogs are different and enjoy different activities. As a baseline, start with simply walking; ensure your dog goes on proper walks with you regularly. Beyond walking do what works best for you and your dog. Go for runs, bike rides, swimming or play fetch. Do whatever is enjoyable and makes the most sense for you and your dog!

General Rules

- Be a leader your dog will follow by being the person you would follow!

- Everything must be earned. Do not give anything away for free. Minimize the amount of unearned affection.

- Use every opportunity available to practice thresholds, i.e. food, crate, doors, etc.

- Only reward the state of mind you want. Do not reinforce unwanted behaviors.

- Deliver consequences with proper timing and appropriate intensity to match the behavior. The consequence needs to be meaningful to your dog.

- Initially, your dog should have limited freedom within the house; using the Place command is a good way to achieve this.

- Having your dog leashed at all times around the house allows you to give a correction anytime you need to.

- Crate your dog when you cannot supervise. Do not allow unwanted behaviors to be created in your absence.

Conclusion

My hope in sharing this information is you will see that transforming the dog you have now into the dog you imagine you could have is not out of reach. If you put in the work establishing leadership, structure, rules, and accountability, the results will far exceed your expectations.

The outline is simple and makes sense, but, the hard part is the follow-through; the discipline to stay committed to reach the end goal and continue with this new way of life indefinitely to ensure lasting change in our dogs and our relationships with them.

It's ok to stumble along the way because that's normal. The important part is to keep your eyes on the bigger picture. Push through and get back to doing the work. If you have questions, are seeking advice, need hands-on training, or just some encouragement to help you along the way please reach out and let me know. I would love to help you reach the end goal and look forward to doing so.

Training Tools

Collars

- Flat buckle collar

  A standard collar. The static nature of the collar does not provide a means for fine control of the pressure applied to the dog's neck when the D-Ring is engaged.

- Martingale collar

  Similar to a standard collar, but designed to tighten around the dog's neck when its D-Ring is engaged. This helps prevent the collar from slipping over the dog's head and allows pressure to be applied from the leash when the collar is engaged.

- Snap-around dog collar

  Similar to a choke collar in that it constricts indefinitely. It is designed to sit high on the dog's neck just behind the jaw.

- Prong collar

  A collar with metal prongs that lays snugly against the dog's neck. It is designed to apply even pressure around the dog's neck when engaged.

- eCollar

  Electronic collar that provides controlled stimulation through contact points that sit against a dog's neck.

Leashes

- Slip lead

  A leash and collar combo that works like a choke chain in that it provides indefinite constriction. It is designed to sit high on the dog's neck just behind the jaw. The slip lead is quick and easy to use and allows for fine control of pressure applied to the dog's neck.

- Leather leash

  A durable leather lead to attach to a collar with a D-Ring. Provides control for direction and discipline.

- Long line

  A long leash (10+ feet) that attaches to a collar with a D-Ring. Allows for control of the dog at a significance distance.

Rewards

- Verbal

  Verbal praise. Yes! Good! Good boy! Good girl! Etc.

- Touch

  Physical touch. Petting.

- Food

  Any desirable food or treat.

- Toys

  Any desirable toy or object.

Aversives

- Pet convincer

  An air canister that delivers a quick burst of air. Typically this is used to break a dog's concentration when they are focused on something they should not be focused on.

- Bonker

  A rolled up towel secured by rubber bands that is thrown toward the dog to break its concentration and stop it from whatever the dog is currently doing.

- eCollar

  An electronic collar that delivers a stim to the dog's neck at the level you specify using the remote control. Typical corrections using an eCollar are relatively low. High corrections are reserved for dangerous behaviors such as biting.

- Bark collar

  An electronic collar that delivers a stim to the dog's neck when the dog barks. These work well at managing excessive barking while you are not home to address it yourself.

Safety

- Muzzle

  A muzzle prevents a dog from biting. A very important tool when dealing with aggressive dogs.

- Crate

  A wire crate that serves as a dog's den. Provides a means to keep a dog comfortable and safe, especially when the dog is alone and unsupervised.

Commands & Skills

Marker Phrases

The foundation of communication between you and your dog will be based on these marker phrases. We will use these phrases to communicate to the dog which behaviors we approve of and which behaviors we disapprove of. Using these simple, yet highly effective, phrases will form the basis from which we can teach our dogs everything they will ever need to know.

Yes – The dog has successfully accomplished the given task!

Good – The dog is successfully accomplishing the given task; keep going – don't stop!

No – The dog has done something that we do not approve of – stop that!

OK – The release; the dog is no longer held to the current command – they are free to move!

Basic Commands

Sit

One of the first commands a dog will learn is Sit. The Sit puts a dog in a stationary position in which the dog is upright, with front legs fully extended, and the dog's rear touching the ground. To achieve this position use a slip lead to apply light vertical pressure while pressing downward on the dog's rear.

Down

The down position is all about putting a dog in a stationary position with a passive, relaxed state of mind. In a down position the dog's belly, rear and elbows will be flush with the ground. To achieve this position use a slip lead to apply downward pressure until the dog lies down.

Stay

The Stay command tells a dog to stay put until they receive further instruction. It can be applied to a Sit or a Down. It is recommended that a dog be taught an implicit stay with their Sit and Down commands, i.e., a dog should assume that when issued a Sit or Down command the dog will stay in that position and location until further instruction is issued.

Come

The Come command is used to recall the dog to your position. Ultimately, the dog should drop everything and come to you. As simple as this concept is, it is the most difficult command to master!

Advanced Commands

Place

We use the place command to put our dog's in a down position in a specific location; controlling the dog's location and creating a calm, relaxed state of mind. Place can be whatever or wherever we want it to be, it should just stand out as a location that is different than the space around it. The dog should not break from place until the release command is issued.

Up

The Up command is used to allow the dog to jump or climb to an elevated location; this can be furniture, such as a bed or couch, or it can be when entering a vehicle.

Off

The Off command is the opposite of the Up command. We use the Off command to tell our dog to move to a lower position. The Off command is great for removing a dog from the bed or couch.

Out

The Out command is used to remove anything that is currently in the dog's mouth in a safe fashion. When we issue the Out command, the dog should release the object in their mouth and step away from it. This is very helpful to avoid harmful objects from being ingested and preventing unnecessary dog bite incidents.

Wait

The Wait command is used as a Pause button; when the Wait command is issued we want our dog to freeze and await our next instruction. Typically, this will be used to aid us in stopping or delaying a dog from performing an action they intended to perform.

Thresholds

Thresholds are invisible barriers; points at which we want our dog to look to us for permission to make the next move.

Crate

- Dog should exit only when given permission

Doorways

- Doorways of consequence, such as the front and back doors of a house
- Dog should pass through doorways only when given permission

Gates

- Dog should pass through gateways only when given permission

Car

- Dog should enter a vehicle only when given permission
- Dog should exit a vehicle only when given permission

Food

- Dog should wait to eat until permission is given

Leash Walking

Heel

- Dog's head/shoulders should be at or behind your leg
- Leash should be loose, but comfortably in your control to give direction or correction in a moment's notice
- Dog should follow your body's direction – forward, stop, left, right
- No sniffing, marking, lunging, or barking while heeling

Recall

Short line

- Initial guidance to give meaning to recall command

Long line

- Increased difficulty but with leash guidance to ensure compliance with command

Long line with eCollar

- Layer eCollar with long line in preparation for offleash recall

Offleash

- Offleash with eCollar

Schedule

Daily Agenda

Activity	Description	Skill(s)
Wake up	Day begins! Dog sleeps in crate overnight.	
Eat	Meal is served in crate. Dog politely waits until given permission to eat.	Threshold
Exercise (Walk/Yard)	Dog waits for permission to exit crate before the morning walk or yard run.	Threshold
Place	Dog is in Place as you get ready for your day.	Command
Crate	Crate dog before you leave for the day.	
Exercise (Walk/Yard)	Dog waits for permission to exit crate before the afternoon walk or yard run.	Threshold
Place	Dog is in Place as you perform your evening tasks, such as unwinding from the day, preparing dinner, etc.	Command
Eat	Meal is served in crate. Dog politely waits until given permission to eat.	Threshold
Exercise (Walk/Yard)	Dog waits for permission to exit crate before the evening walk or yard run.	Threshold
Sleep	End of the day! Dog sleeps in crate overnight.	

Resources

- Prudentk9training.com

Notes

Notes

Notes

Notes